I Love
Cats and Kittens

David Alderton

QED Publishing

Editor: Tasha Percy
In-house Designer: Krina Patel
Art Director: Laura Roberts-Jensen
Designer: Melissa Alaverdy

Copyright © QED Publishing 2014

First published in the UK in 2014 by
QED Publishing
A Quarto Group company
The Old Brewery,
6 Blundell Street,
London, N7 9BH

www.qed-publishing.co.uk

A catalogue record for this book is
available from the British Library.

ISBN 978 1 78171 544 4

Printed in China

Picture credits

(t=top, b=bottom, l=left, r=right, fc=front cover, bc=back cover)

Alamy fc Juniors Bildarchiv GmbH, bc blickwinkel, 4b Juniors Bildarchiv GmbH, 10 MIXA, 13 Juniors Bildarchiv GmbH, 19 Tierfotoagentur, 23tl Juniors Bildarchiv, 23b Tierfotoagentur, 24-25b Tierfotoagentur, 26bl Life on white, 26tr Juniors Bildarchiv GmbH, 26br Petra Wegner, 27b Fikmik, 29 Juniors Bildarchiv GmbH, 30b Juniors Bildarchiv GmbH, 33b Andrew Linscott, 41 Oleg Kozlov, 42b blickwinkel, 47b MJ Photography, 48tl Tierfotoagentur, 48-49b Shotshop GmbH, 49r Tierfotoagentur, 54tl Idamini, 55bl Idamini, 55br Idamini, 56r Juniors Bildarchiv GmbH, 58tr Tierfotoagentur, 58b Tierfotoagentur, 66-67 Juniors Bildarchiv GmbH, 88bl PhotoAlto, 89tr Juniors Bildarchiv GmbH, 90tr Juniors Bildarchiv GmbH, 90br Natalya Onishchenko, 102br Natalya Onishchenko, 103 Tierfotoagentur, 104l Tierfotoagentur, 105br Visions of America, LLC, 114b imagebroker

Animal Photography.com 6tl Helmi Flick, 6tr Helmi Flick, 7tr Helmi Flick, 7b Helmi Flick, 12tl Tetsu Yamazaki , 12b Helmi Flick, 16tl Helmi Flick, 16b Helmi Flick, 17 Helmi Flick, 25r Alan Robinson, 27tr Johnny Kruger, 31 Alan Robinson, 35t Tetsu Yamazaki, 35br Tetsu Yamazaki, 36 Johnny Kruger, 38tr Helmi Flick, 38b Helmi Flick, 43tr Helmi Flick, 43b Helmi Flick, 47tr Johnny Kruger, 52b Sally Anne Thompson, 54b Helmi Flick, 56bl Alan Robinson, 62-63 Helmi Flick, 64tl Leanne Graham, 64tr Helmi Flick, 64br Alan Robinson, 65tr Leanne Graham, 68-69t Sally Anne Thompson, 70-71tr Tetsu Yamazaki, 71b Tetsu Yamazaki, 76t Helmi Flick, 77b Helmi Flick, 82-83t Vidar Skauen, 83r Vidar Skauen, 84t, Helmi Flick, 84b Helmi Flick, 85l Tetsu Yamazaki, 85br Helmi Flick, 87 Tetsu Yamazaki, 94tl Tetsu Yamazaki, 94b Alan Robinson, 96t Tetsu Yamazaki, 98tl Tetsu Yamazaki, 98-99b Helmi Flick, 99tl Helmi Flick, 99r Tetsu Yamazaki, 102l Helmi Flick, 104-105t Helmi Flick, 106-107t Helmi Flick, 106-107b Alan Robinson, 107r Alan Robinson, 108-109b Helmi Flick, 109t Helmi Flick, 110l Tetsu Yamazaki, 110br Alan Robinson, 111 Tetsu Yamazaki, 112l Alan Robinson, 112-113t Helmi Flick, 112br Tetsu Yamazaki, 113b Vidar Skauen, 115t Tetsu Yamazaki, 116-117 Tetsu Yamazaki, 118tr Johnny Kruger, 118b Johnny Kruger, 119 Tetsu Yamazaki

Ardea.com 8tl Jean-Michel Labat, 9 Jean Michel Labat, 25tl Jean Michel Labat, 26tl Jean Michel Labat, 28b Jean-Michel Labat, 34tr Jean Michel Labat, 34-35b Jean Michel Labat, 37tr Jean Michel Labat, 39 Jean-Michel Labat, 42t John Daniels, 44tl Jean-Michel Labat, 45t Jean-Michel Labat, 46 Jean-Michel Labat, 56br Jean-Michel Labat, 70tl Jean-Michel Labat, 70bl Jean-Michel Labat, 115b Jean-Michel Labat

Corbis 30tl Rachel McKenna/cultura, 100-101 D. Sheldon/FI Online

DK Images 69tr Dave King

FLPA 11t Mitsuaki Iwago/Minden Pictures, 11b Gerard Lacz, 14 Ramona Richter/Tierfotoagentur, 15tr Ramona Richter/Tierfotoagentur, 15b Ramona Richter/Tierfotoagentur, 20-21b PICANI/Imagebroker, 22tlPICANI/Imagebroker, 24tl Ramona Richter/Tierfotoagentur, 28tl Jana Weichelt/Tierfotoagentur, 33tr Chris Brignell, 48bl ImageBroker/Imagebroker, 53 Gerard Lacz. 57b Gerard Lacz, 59r PICANI/Imagebroker, 60tl S. Schwerdtfeger/Tierfotoagentur, 60bl S. Schwerdtfeger/Tierfotoagentur, 72-73 / Imagebroker, 74b ImageBroker/Imagebroker, 76b Ramona Richter/Tierfotoagentur, 77tr Ramona Richter/Tierfotoagentur, 91 Jana Weichelt/Tierfotoagentur, 92 PICANI/Imagebroker, 93tl PICANI/Imagebroker, 93b PICANI/Imagebroker, 108t Tui De Roy/Minden Pictures, 109br Tui De Roy/Minden Pictures, 114tl Chris Brignell

Getty Images 120 Marc Henrie
Istockphoto.com 37b BenAkiba, 45br fotojagodka
Nature Photo Library 32 Jane Burton
Photoshot.com 18tr NHPA, 18b Credit: Juniors Tierbildarchiv, 69b NHPA

Shutterstock 4t Hein Nouwens, 4tl ingret, 4-5 Maximus256, 5 Denys Dolnikov, 6b Nataliya Kuznetsova, , 8b Robynrg, 20tl Utekhina Anna, 21tl HelleM, 21tr Eric Isselee, 22bl Bildagentur Zoonar GmbH, 40tr j-paul, 40b Aliaksei Smalenski, 44bl dezi, 44-45b ADA_photo, 49tl Eric Isselee, 50 kimberrywood, 51tr Eric Isselee, 51bl ArjaKo's, 52tr Eric Isselee, 55t SUSAN LEGGETT, 57tr dien, 61t ingret, 61b alexkar08, 64bl Linn Currie, 65b Linn Currie, 68b Cindi Wilson, 74tr Joanna22, 75t hosphotos, 75b Joop Snijder Photography, 78tl Linn Currie, 78r Eric Isselee, 79tl Bildagentur Zoonar GmbH, 79tr Eric Isselee, 79b Bildagentur Zoonar GmbH, 80t Linn Currie, 80b absolutimages, 81b WilleeCole, 81tr Eric Isselee, 82-83b Toloubaev Stanislav, 86tl Scampi, 86bl Tetsu Yamazaki, 86br Tatiana Makotra, 88t Anneka, 88br Eric Isselee, 89b Linn Currie, 90bl Gita Kulinitch Studio, 95 Nikita Starichenko, 96b Utekhina Anna, 97tr Tetsu Yamazaki, 97l Alan Robinson, 104-105b Krissi Lundgren, 106bl A. Vasilyev

Contents

Abyssinian

The founding cat of this breed was brought back from the East African country of Abyssinia, which is now known as Ethiopia. Abyssinians have a special type of tabby markings. This makes their coat look rather sparkly. They are very friendly cats that enjoy playing.

American Bobtail

The American Bobtail has a much shorter tail than most cats, measuring between a half and a third of their length. This breed is often shorthaired, with tabby markings. All of today's American Bobtails are related to an abandoned kitten found in the state of Arizona, USA.

American Curl

The curly ears of these cats are really unusual! There is a choice of short and longer coated American Curls, both of which have quite slim bodies. These cats are descended from a stray that moved in with a Californian couple in 1981.

American Shorthair

Descended from street cats, the American Shorthair can now be seen at many cat shows. It is a strong, muscular cat, bred in a wide range of colours and patterns. American Shorthairs with tabby markings are most common. They are friendly cats by nature.

American Wirehair

Here is a cat whose coat feels very different, having an unusual wiry feel. The hairs, including the whiskers, may be curled. The first American Wirehair cat was bred on a farm in Upstate New York, USA, and even today, these cats are rare. Their unusual coat needs no special care.

Angora

Active and lively, the Angora has been developed from crossings of Abyssinian and Siamese cats. Angoras have quite long bodies, with soft, silky coats. Their fur is longer on the body than the face, and does not mat, or tangle, easily. Angoras enjoy chasing after toys.

15

Australian Mist

The first cats of this breed were spotted, but now there are others with marbled patterning. The markings on the coat of the Australian Mist are not that clear. They appear rather misty, and that's how they got their name. These are gentle cats, and tend not to scratch, nor are they keen on hunting.

Balinese

These elegant cats are the longhaired form of the Siamese breed, and they have similar patterning, with stunning blue eyes. They have a thin coat, and this helps to emphasise their athletic body. Balinese like climbing and jumping.

Bengal

This breed is the result of matings between wild Asian Leopard Cats and domestic cats. This explains why Bengals often keep their tail close to the ground when walking, like wild cats. They love climbing and are often fascinated with water too. They enjoy trying to catch the drops from a dripping tap.

Birman

There is no mistaking a Birman, because of its unusual markings. It has white areas on its front feet, known as gloves. White fur also extends up the back of the legs, and these markings are called boots. Whatever their actual coat colour, Birmans always have blue eyes.

Bombay

Looking just like a miniature black panther, the Bombay has jet black, glossy fur. Its eyes are usually coppery in colour, but sometimes green. These are easy cats to look after, but may be greedy, putting on weight. Bombays are happy living with dogs.

British Longhair

These cats are the longhaired form of the British Shorthair, and so their coats will need more grooming and care. British Longhairs can be bred in a similarly wide range of colours and patterns to its short-coated cousin, and have the same laid-back personality.

British Shorthair

This breed was developed from ordinary street cats, and over time, new colours were created. Almost every colour and pattern that you can think of in cats can now be seen in this breed. British Shorthairs have become much larger than ordinary pet cats. They are intelligent, friendly and playful.

Burmese

As a result of differences in their ancestry, Burmese in North America now have more rounded faces than those seen in Europe. You can choose Burmese in a range of colours; their eyes normally vary from yellowish to gold. They are good as indoor cats and play well with dogs and children.

Burmilla

Bred for its friendly nature as much as its beautiful colouring, the Burmilla is a great choice of pet. Its coat really does sparkle as it moves. Its name reflects the two breeds from which it was bred in 1981. These were the Burmese and the Chinchilla Longhair.

California Spangled

The aim of Paul Casey, who created this unusual breed, was to develop a domestic cat with a spotted coat that looked and walked like a small leopard. He hoped it would remind people of how the wild relatives of domestic cats were becoming threatened in the wild.

Chartreux

The greyish fur – known as blue in the cat world – is a main feature of the ancient Chartreux breed. In fact, this is the only colour these cats come in. They are Europe's oldest cat breed, whose ancestors have lived at the same monastery in France for over 800 years.

Chausie

These cats are bigger than ordinary domestic cats. This is because they are descended partly from the jungle cat, a wild species that played a part in their early breeding. Chausies can jump the height of a person, and run along branches, being very active cats.

Cornish Rex

A litter of farm cats born during 1950 in the county of Cornwall, southwestern England, included a kitten with an unusual very short, curly coat. He was named Kallibunker, and became the founder of the Cornish Rex breed. These cats will sit up on their hindlegs, just like dogs.

Cymric

This is the longhaired form of the Manx cat, and as a result, some Cymrics have no trace of a tail. The Cymric has an easy-going, playful nature, and will live happily in a home with a dog. It has a reputation for having a long lifespan.

Devon Rex

These elf-like cats have mischievous natures, and love playing games, such as chasing after balls. They soon learn to recognize the sound of their names, coming when called. Their soft, thin coat means that they can feel the cold. They do not enjoy going outdoors in bad weather.

Egyptian Mau

Egypt in the Middle East is where cats became popular pets thousands of years ago. This breed is descended from the street cats there, and has a spotted tabby pattern. The word '*mau*' means 'cat' in Egyptian, and probably comes from the 'miaow' sound that cats make.

European Shorthair

Bred from the street cats of Europe, the European Shorthair is hardy and friendly by nature, and adaptable too. Their short coats need little grooming, and they can be seen in many colours and patterns. European Shorthairs usually live happily alongside dogs that share their home.

50

Exotic Shorthair

Looking rather like a teddy bear, with its flattish face, big round eyes and cuddly coat, the Exotic is the result of breeding between Persian Longhairs and American Shorthairs. It has now become very popular, especially in North America, and can be seen in a wide range of coloured and patterned varieties.

Havana Brown

This cat is an attractive warm, chocolate-brown shade, matching that of a Havana cigar. Its eyes are always green and oval in shape. Lively and playful, the Havana Brown is a relative of the Siamese, and has a similar athletic build.

Highlander

This breed is very easy to recognize, because it has slightly curled ears, combined with a short bobtail. Highlanders exist in almost any colour or pattern, and they can have long or short fur. They love to play and have lots of energy!

Japanese Bobtail

These cats are often black and white, or tortoiseshell and white, although they are bred in other colours too. They have unusual pompom tails. Their habit of sitting in windows with a paw raised inspired the Japanese tradition of placing a ceramic ornament called '*Maneki Neko*' – meaning the 'Beckoning Cat' – in windows to greet visitors.

Korat

This ancient breed comes from the northeastern province of Korat, Thailand. The Korat has a distinctive silvery-blue coat. Young cats have yellowish eyes, which change to a beautiful shade of green. These cats were traditionally given in pairs as wedding gifts to wish couples good luck.

Kurilian Bobtail

The homeland of these rare cats is the Kuril Islands, lying between Russia and Japan. It is thought that they are descended from cats taken there by sailors from mainland Asia many centuries ago. They have a large head, and tabby patterning, as well as a short bobtail.

Lambkin

With fur that can look rather like lamb's wool, this breed has the coat of a Selkirk Rex combined with the short legs of a Munchkin. These cats can climb very well, both in the home and outdoors in the garden, and are affectionate by nature.

LaPerm

All of today's LaPerms trace their ancestry back to a farm cat born in 1982 on a fruit farm in Oregon, USA. These cats have loose, bouncy fur, with longhaired members of this breed having bigger coats. LaPerm kittens are often quite bald at birth, as their fur tends to grow slowly.

Maine Coon

This was the first breed developed in the USA, in the state of Maine. During the 1800s, these cats were commonly kept on farms. Today, the Maine Coon has become the most popular cat breed in the world. Male kittens grow larger than females.

Manx

Hundreds of years ago, cats on the Isle of Man, off England's northwestern coast, started to give birth to kittens without tails. The Manx can be bred in many colours, often having white areas in their coats. These cats are playful and intelligent by nature. Manx have featured on the island's coinage and stamps.

Munchkin

These cats are a new breed and can be easily recognized by their short legs. There are both short and long-coated forms. People used to worry that the short legs would handicap these cats, but this has not proved to be a problem. They can run fast, although they will not jump far.

71

Nebelung

Kittens of this breed are born with blue eyes, but these change in colour to green or sometimes yellowish-green. The distinctive blue-grey coat of a Nebelung has a silky texture, and is of medium length. They are related to the Russian breed and are currently quite rare.

Norwegian Forest Cat

Bred to survive in the bitterly cold winters of Norway, these are large cats, with dense, water-repellent coats. They shed their thick fur in spring, losing their ruff – the area of long fur under the chin. Tabbies are common. These cats like to roam around outside.

75

Ocicat

The stunning appearance of wild cats has often attracted breeders who want to create domestic cats with similar patterning. In this case, a breed was developed that displayed the spotted markings of the Ocelot, which lives in parts of Central and South America.

Oriental

These cats exist in more colours and patterns than any other breed. There are hundreds of possible varieties – some of which have not even been developed yet! Orientals are playful, active and vocal cats, with large ears and an elegant body shape.

Persian

This cat dates back to the late 1800s, and was one of the first recognized purebreds. Aside from their long coats, which require a lot of grooming to prevent the hair from becoming matted, Persians have short noses and small ears too. They exist in many different colours and patterns.

Peterbald

This relatively new breed was created in St Petersburg, Russia, in 1993. The coat length of these cats varies widely. The whiskers can be curly in some cases too. In terms of body shape, the Peterbald looks rather like a Siamese cat.

Pixiebob

This unusual breed resembles a miniature Bobcat, as reflected by its very short tail and build. Pixiebobs are often brown tabbies. They may look like wild cats, but DNA tests have shown that they are simply domestic cats.

Ragamuffin

Ragamuffins are large cats that have been carefully bred to ensure they are gentle by nature, just like their ancestor, the Ragdoll. They have been created in a wide range of colours and patterns. Their long coats do not mat easily, and are very soft.

Ragdoll

The name of these cats comes from the way that they relax when they are picked up, lying in your arms like a ragdoll. They are also one of the few breeds that display little if any hunting instincts, meaning that they will not harm wildlife.

Russian

These cats were developed around the port of Archangel, in the far north of Russia, and from here they were first taken to England and other European countries in the 1860s. They were known for a time both as the Archangel and Russian Blue, but other colours such as white now exist too.

Savannah

Named after the plains of Africa, these cats are hybrids – being the result of matings between the wild Serval and domestic cats. They are the largest breed, much bigger than ordinary cats, and have spotted patterning. They may greet people by bouncing up to them, rather like a dog!

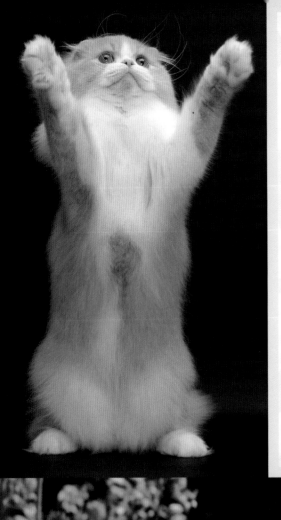

Scottish Fold

The cute appearance of these cats stems not just from the way that their ears are folded down, but also the rounded shape of their face. The first Scottish Fold kitten, called Susie, cropped up on a farm in Scotland in 1961. There are now long and short-haired forms of these affectionate cats.

95

Selkirk Rex

Descended from an abandoned kitten brought into a rescue shelter in Montana, USA, this breed is named after the nearby Selkirk Mountains. It is a typical Rex breed, with a curly coat, and exists in both short and long-coated varieties. They are quite large cats with round faces.

Serengeti

This breed does not come from the Serengeti region of East Africa, as its name might suggest. Breeders wanted to develop a cat that looked like the Serval. Rather than using wild cats of any kind, the Serengeti has been developed from Oriental and Bengal bloodlines. Serengetis are friendly, spotted and relatively long-legged cats.

Siamese

Sleek, short-coated and noisy, the Siamese is one of the best-known breeds. Kittens are born white, and only develop the darker areas of colouration on their legs, feet, face, ears and tail over time. These areas of the body are described as the points.

Siberian

Well-protected against the freezing cold of the Siberian winter, these cats roamed the countryside for hundreds of years before they came to the attention of cat breeders. As with many longhaired cats, their coat becomes thicker and longer during the winter, and then is shed in spring.

Singapura

The ancestors of this breed were discovered living wild in the Asian country of Singapore. They became known locally as 'drain cats' because they used to shelter in storm drains. The Singapura is a ticked tabby. This means Singapuras have alternating dark brown and ivory-white banding running down their hairs. They are also one of the smallest breeds of cat.

Snowshoe

White markings on the front feet help to identify the snowshoe. A white stripe is present, extending between the eyes and broadening over the nose and around the jaws. This is known as a blaze. The eyes are blue, reflecting the part played by the Siamese in the breed's ancestry.

Sokoke

This breed is named after the Sokoke forest region in Kenya, Africa, where the ancestors of this breed were discovered in 1978. Their patterning is very distinct, as is their behaviour. They often walk on tiptoe, and the male cat helps the female to take care of their kittens.

Somali

Somalis are the long-coated form of the Abyssinian breed, and they are similar in nature. If you look closely at their coat, you will see alternating light and dark bands of colour extending along the length of their hairs. The Somali is a cautious breed that loves to play and share cuddles.

Sphynx

Although sometimes called the hairless cat, the Sphynx can have traces of hair present on its body. These cats are not only at risk from the cold – they can suffer sunburn easily too, particularly where there are pink areas of skin, and so they are generally best kept indoors.

Tonkinese

Related to both the Burmese and the Siamese, the Tonkinese has a pale body, often with a darker face and feet. The shading on the body darkens over time. Its head is more rounded and less triangular in appearance than a Siamese, and this is how they can be told apart.

Toyger

This domestic cat looks just like a miniature tiger, with stripes on the sides of its body. Its ears are quite large and its tail is long. The founder of this new breed is a street cat from Kashmir, India.

Turkish Angora

These cats have been kept in the area of Angora, Turkey, for thousands of years. They are often white in colour, and were probably the ancestor of the Persian Longhair. Their coat has a very distinctive, silky texture, but they do not have a thick undercoat.

Turkish Van

This breed is found around Lake Van in Turkey. Although many people think cats dislike water, Turkish Van cats often go swimming in the lake in summer to cool down when it is very hot.